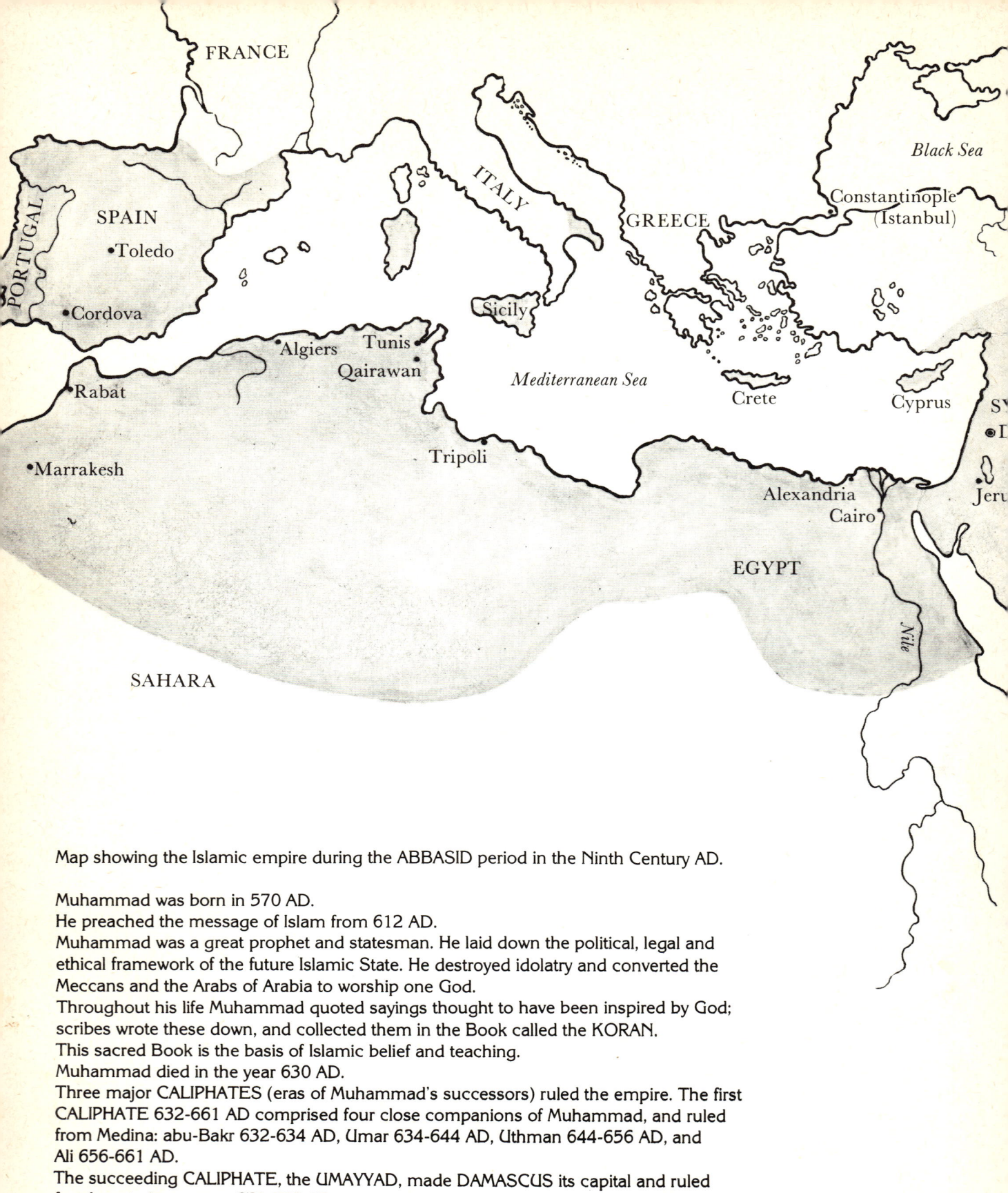

Map showing the Islamic empire during the ABBASID period in the Ninth Century AD.

Muhammad was born in 570 AD.
He preached the message of Islam from 612 AD.
Muhammad was a great prophet and statesman. He laid down the political, legal and ethical framework of the future Islamic State. He destroyed idolatry and converted the Meccans and the Arabs of Arabia to worship one God.
Throughout his life Muhammad quoted sayings thought to have been inspired by God; scribes wrote these down, and collected them in the Book called the KORAN.
This sacred Book is the basis of Islamic belief and teaching.
Muhammad died in the year 630 AD.
Three major CALIPHATES (eras of Muhammad's successors) ruled the empire. The first CALIPHATE 632-661 AD comprised four close companions of Muhammad, and ruled from Medina: abu-Bakr 632-634 AD, Umar 634-644 AD, Uthman 644-656 AD, and Ali 656-661 AD.
The succeeding CALIPHATE, the UMAYYAD, made DAMASCUS its capital and ruled for almost ninety years 661-750 AD.
It was overthrown by the ABBASID CALIPHATE 750-1258 AD which lasted for more than five hundred years, ruling from BAGHDAD.
It was during this time, in the Ninth Century, that the CALIPH ABDULLAH al-MAMOUN ruled this vast empire.

a Prince of Islam

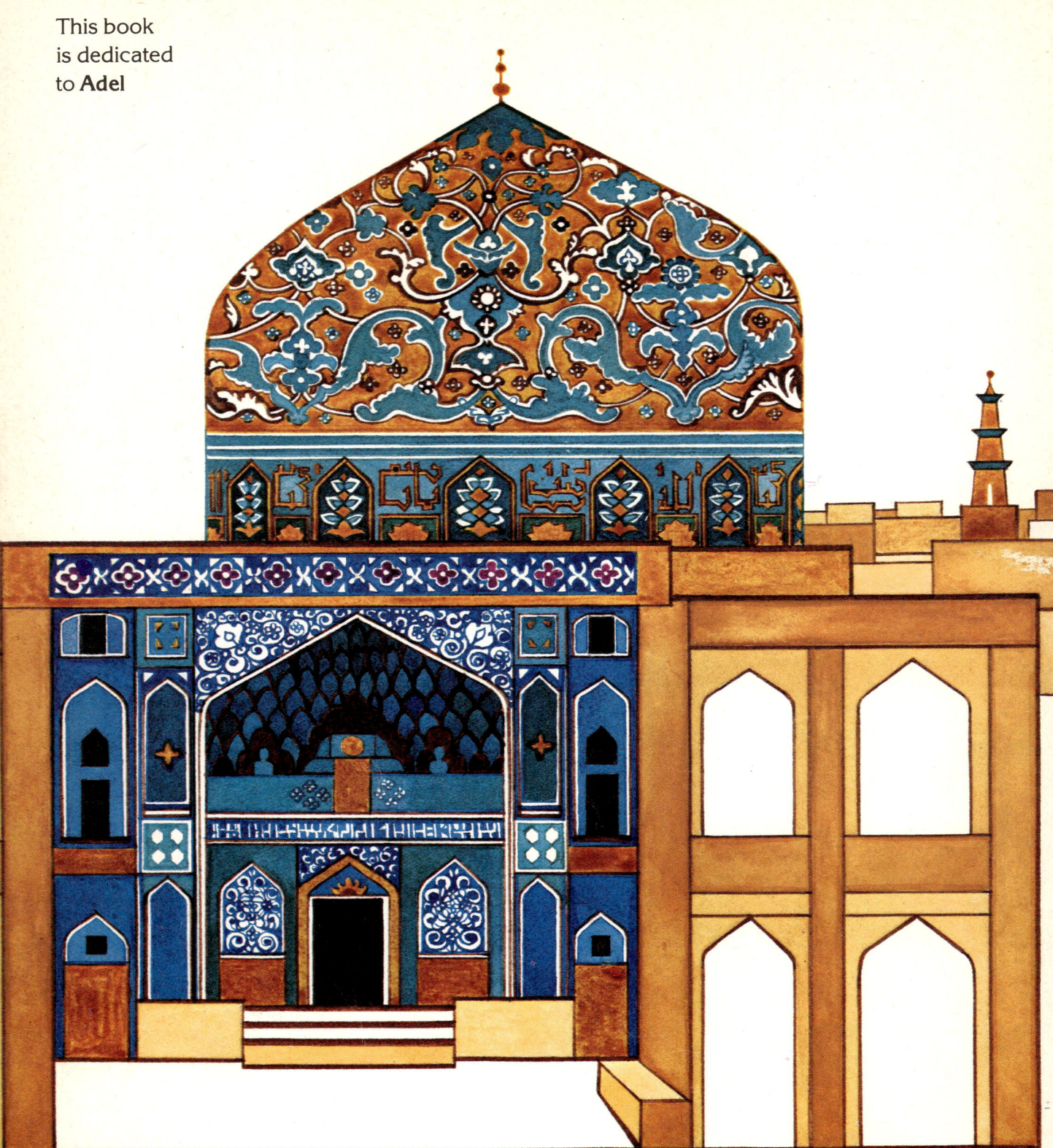

This book is dedicated to **Adel**

First published in the United States in 1977 by Addison-Wesley. Printed in Great Britain. All rights reserved. No part of this book may be reproduced in any form without written permission from Addison-Wesley Publishing Company, Inc., Reading, Massachusetts 01867.

© Carol Barker 1976. First published in Great Britain in 1976 by Macdonald and Jane's (Publishers) Limited

Library of Congress Cataloging in Publication Data

Barker, Carol.
  A prince of Islam.

  (Carol Barker's Worlds of yesterday)
  SUMMARY: Simple text and illustrations describe the childhood and training of a young boy whose father is Caliph of the Muslim Empire in the ninth century.
  [1. Civilization, Islamic — Fiction] I. Title.
PZ7.B2504Pr   [E]   75-45479
ISBN 0-201-00424-0

CAROL BARKER'S WORLDS OF YESTERDAY

a Prince of Islam

ADDISON-WESLEY

In 820 AD Caliph Abdullah al-Mamoun was the ruler of the Muslim Empire. He lived in Baghdad, the capital of Iraq.

In this year the Caliph married.

It was a huge wedding. Each guest was given a present — an estate, a race horse or a slave. Money was poured from the palace walls for the people of Baghdad.

There was music and dancing and feasting.

The Caliph's empire stretched from India to Spain, and he invited the wisest of all races and religions to Baghdad. He found men who could tell wonderful tales and men who knew about the stars. Baghdad became a city where all was new and exciting.

Life was very different for the Caliph's wife, Monya. Muslim women were hidden from all men but their husbands. Husbands had many wives. Monya lived with the Caliph's other wives in the palace harem. They had everything they wanted — even gardens and a pool for hot days.

Here a son was born to Monya and her husband. They named him Omar.

Omar grew up in the harem, playing with the other children. When he was old enough, he learned to swim and to ride. Sometimes his mother told him stories about Muhammad, the founder of the Muslim religion.

Muhammad was born in 570 AD in the city of Mecca in Arabia. Muhammad grew up and married and worked as a merchant until he was forty-two. Then, one day, he heard the Angel Gabriel speaking to him. "You are the messenger of God," said the angel. "You must spread his word."

His sayings were written in the Koran, the Bible of the Muslims. One of his followers, Abu Bakr, became the first Caliph. He wanted to spread the message of the Koran into all lands, thus the wars that built the Muslim Empire began.

Omar wanted to visit Mecca one day. Every Muslim hopes to visit the holy city.

A learned old man, called al-Khwarizmi, taught Omar. He taught him about the generals who had fought the wars.

Omar imagined how the camel troops swept down on their enemies through clouds of desert sand, like the Bedouin tribes.

Sometimes Omar would put on the old torn clothes of a beggar; then he and a servant, Abu, would creep secretly out of the palace into the city streets. Baghdad was filled with street markets and bazaars.

Down at the docks, goods from every corner of the Empire were unloaded — silks, perfumes, porcelain, dyes, spices, precious stones, furs and ivory tusks. Other ships loaded rice, linen, pearls and glass and sailed for places as far away as Russia.

But the most exciting sight for Omar was the market camp of the Bedouins.

Omar knew that the sons of past Caliphs had learned how to survive in the desert, how to travel fast and to fight by living for a time with the Bedouins. He begged his father to let him go. Finally Abdullah al-Mamoun agreed. Omar would visit a Bedouin tribe for three months.

He quickly learned how to ride a camel. The children of the Sheikh, the Bedouin leader, showed him how to set up skin tents when they stopped beside an oasis each evening. The shepherds taught him to care for sheep. He learned how to carve a flute from bamboo and how to play it. He ate what the Bedouins ate — milk, dates and flat, round bread.

Omar liked the evenings best. The Bedouins sat around their fires under the cold stars and sang songs and told tales of battles.

Three months were soon over. Omar was sad to leave his friends and the desert life.

When Omar was ten, he was old enough to make the long trip to Mecca.

The whole family traveled together, the Caliph, his wives, their children, their servants, some nobles, a guard, even musicians to entertain them.

The journey took six weeks.

On the final night they camped outside the city. Next morning they dressed in white pilgrim robes and entered the holy city.

They went into the sacred place, the Kaaba.

Afterward they visited Mount Arafat. There they offered sheep and camels to God.

As Omar lay down to sleep that night, he remembered the story of Muhammad and hoped that he would grow up to be a wise leader of his people. He thought, "I have had a dream, and I have made it come true."

Today there are about 500 million Muslims in the world.

This story goes back to the great age of the Islamic Empire. The Caliph Abdullah al-Mamoun and his wife are historical characters. Omar did not actually exist, although his life in the story is based on events that happened at that time in history.

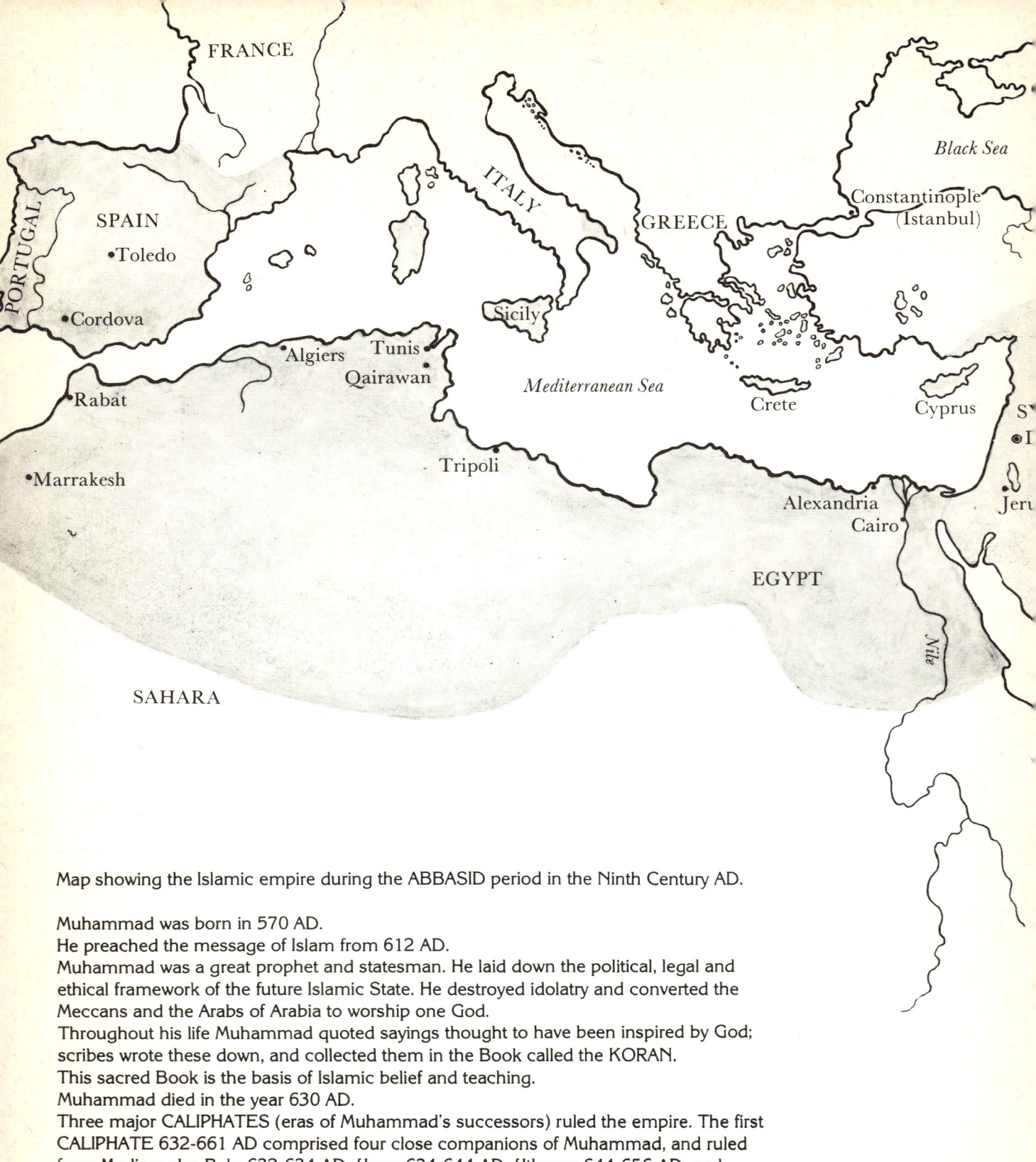

Map showing the Islamic empire during the ABBASID period in the Ninth Century AD.

Muhammad was born in 570 AD.
He preached the message of Islam from 612 AD.
Muhammad was a great prophet and statesman. He laid down the political, legal and ethical framework of the future Islamic State. He destroyed idolatry and converted the Meccans and the Arabs of Arabia to worship one God.
Throughout his life Muhammad quoted sayings thought to have been inspired by God; scribes wrote these down, and collected them in the Book called the KORAN.
This sacred Book is the basis of Islamic belief and teaching.
Muhammad died in the year 630 AD.
Three major CALIPHATES (eras of Muhammad's successors) ruled the empire. The first CALIPHATE 632-661 AD comprised four close companions of Muhammad, and ruled from Medina: abu-Bakr 632-634 AD, Umar 634-644 AD, Uthman 644-656 AD, and Ali 656-661 AD.
The succeeding CALIPHATE, the UMAYYAD, made DAMASCUS its capital and ruled for almost ninety years 661-750 AD.
It was overthrown by the ABBASID CALIPHATE 750-1258 AD which lasted for more than five hundred years, ruling from BAGHDAD.
It was during this time, in the Ninth Century, that the CALIPH ABDULLAH al-MAMOUN ruled this vast empire.

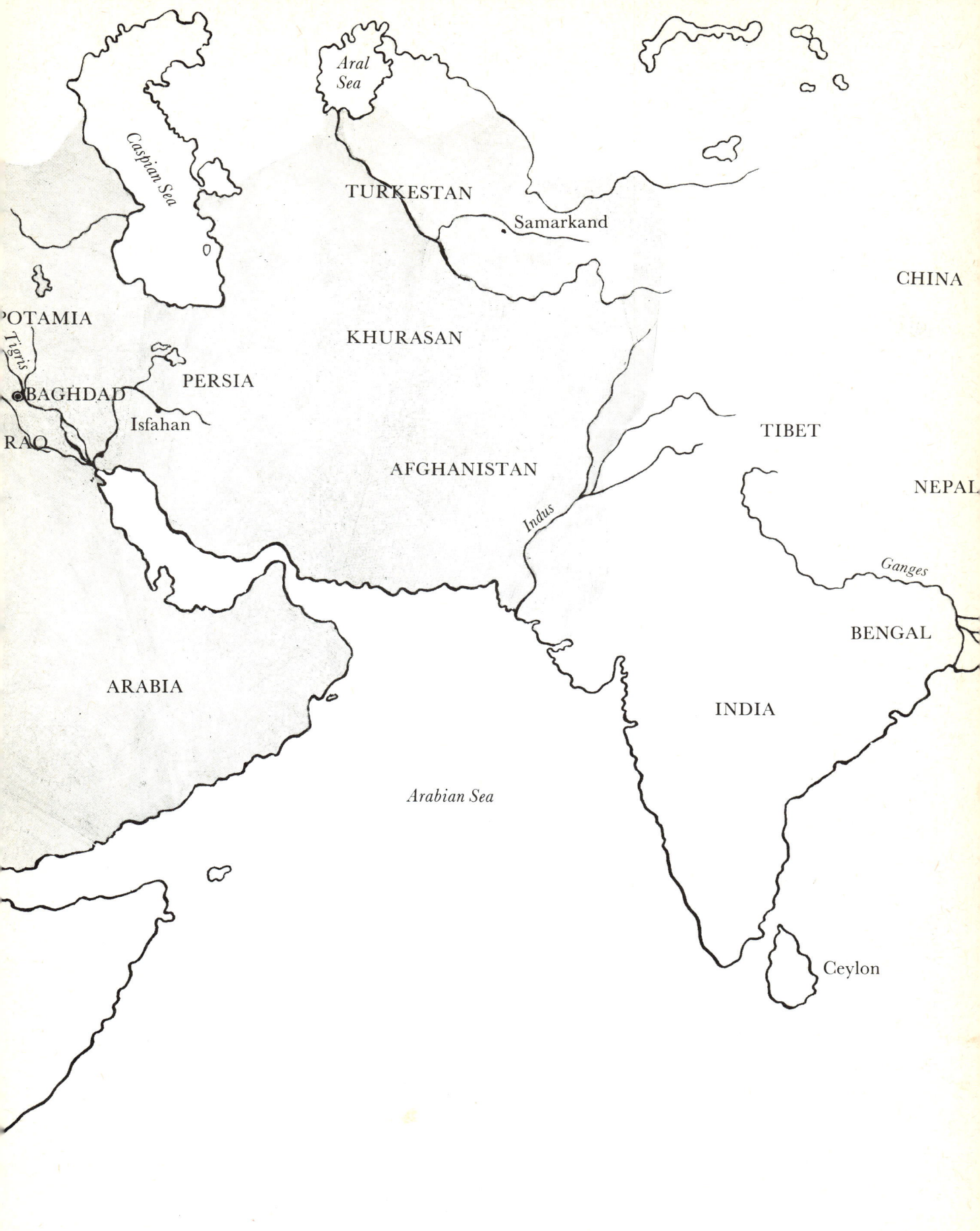